Critters and Kids

Clip Art for the Classroom

Peter Rehnberg

Cottonwood Press, Inc.
Fort Collins, CO

How to use this book

Use the drawings in *Critters and Kids* to perk up homework assignments, tests, lessons, letters home to parents, overhead transparencies, invitations — anything that you want to receive some special attention or a second look. Simply cut out an image in the size you want and secure it to your document. (For best results, use the removable kind of glue stick.) Then photocopy.

If the cut edges of your drawing show on the photocopy, use correction fluid to white out the edges on the copy. (Use correction fluid designed for photocopies so that the ink won't smear.) Then photocopy again.

It's a good idea to clip a large envelope inside the back cover of this book. Then you can keep the cut-out drawings to use again and again.

Enjoy!

Copyright © 2000 by Cottonwood Press, Inc.

The purchaser of *Critters and Kids* may use the original artwork in the book for any school-related print project, such as classroom assignments, newsletters, tests, posters, memos, visual aids, announcements, etc. However, no more than ten drawings may be used for any single publication or project without permission of the publisher. Also, the drawings may not be reprinted, redistributed or resyndicated as stock art or as part of a clip art book or collection, either printed or electronic.

Requests for permission should be addressed to:

Cottonwood Press, Inc.
107 Cameron Drive
Fort Collins, CO 80525
800-864-4297

ISBN 1-877673-41-2

Printed in the United States of America

WRITING — 3
© 2000 Cottonwood Press, Inc. • Fort Collins, CO

6 — READING
© 2000 Cottonwood Press, Inc. • Fort Collins, CO

READING — 7

© 2000 Cottonwood Press, Inc. • Fort Collins, CO

10 — MUSIC/BAND
© 2000 Cottonwood Press, Inc. • Fort Collins, CO

MUSIC/BAND — 11

© 2000 Cottonwood Press, Inc. • Fort Collins, CO

14 — SCIENCE
© 2000 Cottonwood Press, Inc. • Fort Collins, CO

SCIENCE — 15

© 2000 Cottonwood Press, Inc. • Fort Collins, CO

18 — SPORTS

© 2000 Cottonwood Press, Inc. • Fort Collins, CO

SPORTS — 19
© 2000 Cottonwood Press, Inc. • Fort Collins, CO

22 — SPORTS
© 2000 Cottonwood Press, Inc. • Fort Collins, CO

SPORTS — 23
© 2000 Cottonwood Press, Inc. • Fort Collins, CO

COMPUTERS — 27
© 2000 Cottonwood Press, Inc. • Fort Collins, CO

30 — MISCELLANEOUS KIDS/CRITTERS
© 2000 Cottonwood Press, Inc. • Fort Collins, CO

MISCELLANEOUS KIDS/CRITTERS — 31
© 2000 Cottonwood Press, Inc. • Fort Collins, CO

34 — MONSTERS
© 2000 Cottonwood Press, Inc. • Fort Collins, CO

38 — ANIMAL MESSAGES
© 2000 Cottonwood Press, Inc. • Fort Collins, CO

BRIEF NOTES — 39

© 2000 Cottonwood Press, Inc. • Fort Collins, CO

BRIEF NOTES — 43
© 2000 Cottonwood Press, Inc. • Fort Collins, CO

HANDS — 47

© 2000 Cottonwood Press, Inc. • Fort Collins, CO

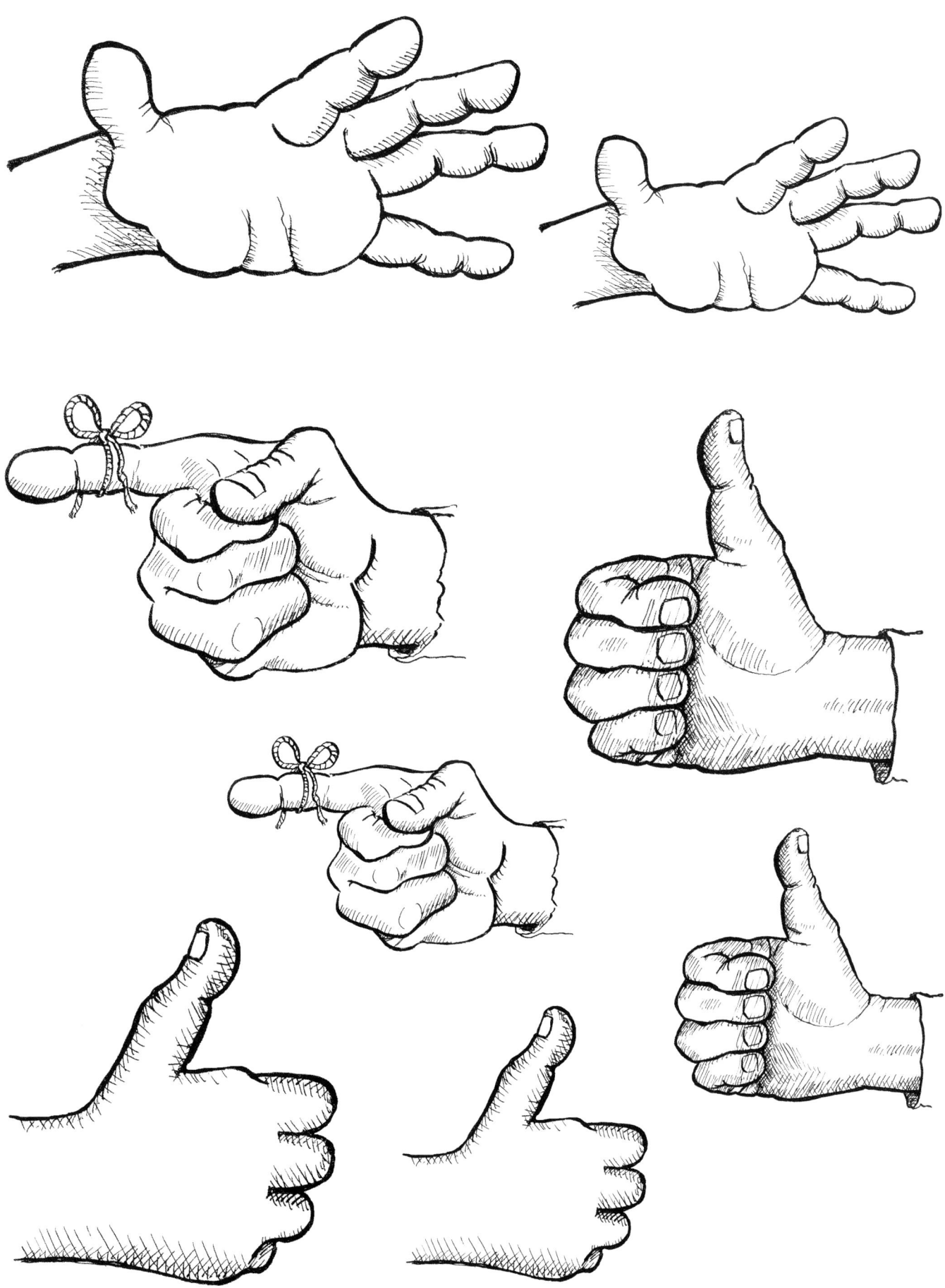

SHAPES — 51
© 2000 Cottonwood Press, Inc. • Fort Collins, CO

54 — BLANK NOTES
© 2000 Cottonwood Press, Inc. • Fort Collins, CO

BLANK NOTES — 55
© 2000 Cottonwood Press, Inc. • Fort Collins, CO

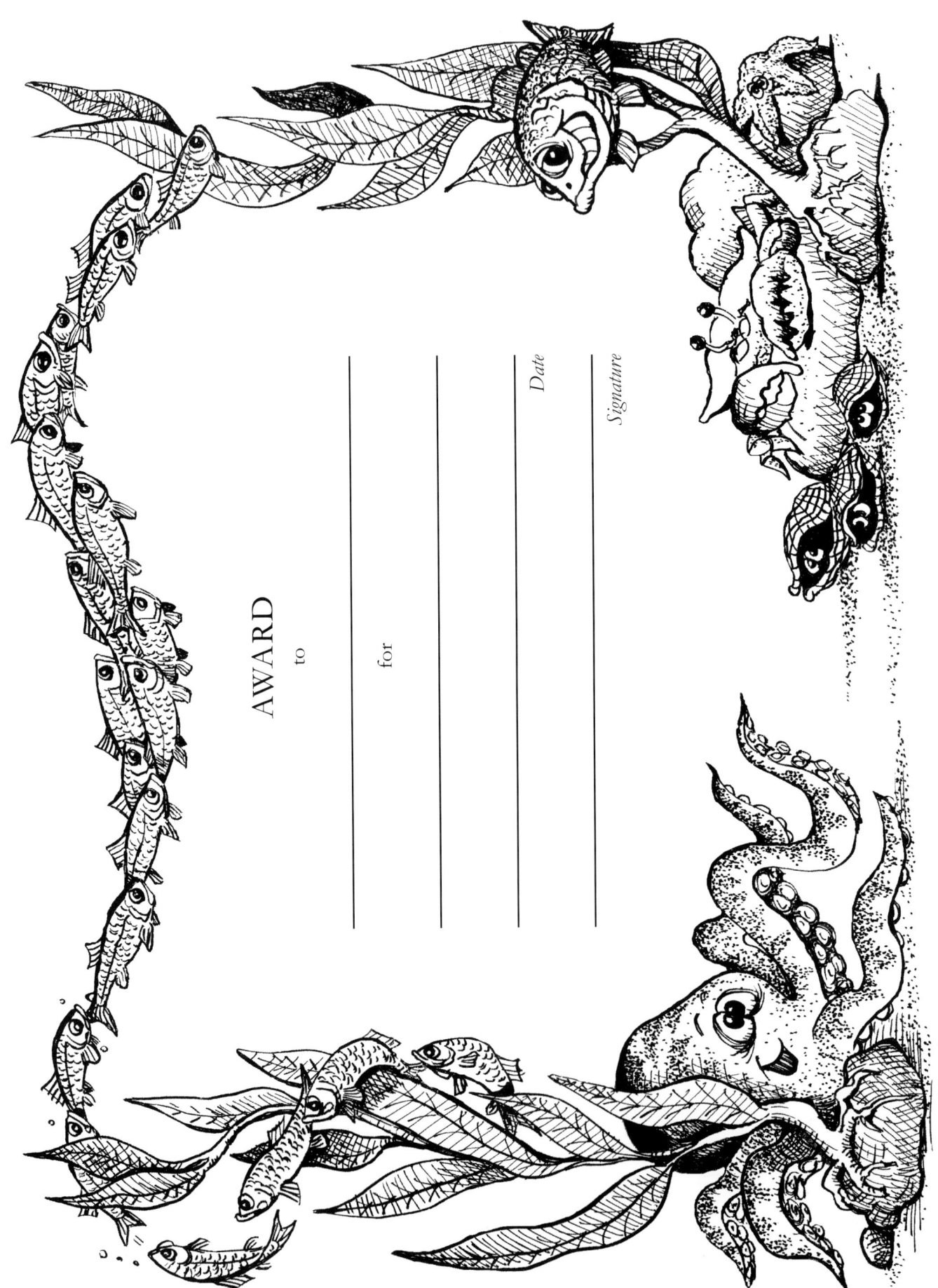